Picture Credits
Ann Ronan Picture Library: 8 (all), 9 (both); **Associated Press:** 59 (top)/Mike Siegel; **Colorific:** 21
(bottom)/Marcus Brooke: **Gamma:** 4-5/Kashi, 16/Kashi, 27/Halstead, 29/Francis Aspesteguy, 41, 42-43/
Halstead, 52-53 (main pic)/Halstead, 54-55/Halstead, 58/Francis Apesteguy, 59 (bottom)/Luc Novovitch;
Images Colour Library: 18, 34-35, 51, 60; **Image Select:** 19, 23 (top), 39 (top); **Lakeside School:** 12,
13/Rex Ziak, 15 (top), 15 (bottom)/Rex Ziak; **Katz:** 52 (bottom)/Mcvay/Saba/Rea; **Microsoft:** 24, 45, 50, 53
(both), 56 (both), 57 (all); **Rex Features:** 20-21 (main pic), 21 (top)/Charles Sykes), 47; **Spectrum Colour
Library:** 11/D and J Heaton; **Sygma:** 7/Joe McNally; **Zefa:** 23 (bottom)/H.R. Bramaz, 31, 39 (bottom),
40, 46, 48.

The Publishers have been unable to contact the copyright holder of the photographic illustrations on pages 10,
25, 32, 49 and would be grateful for any information.

The Publishers have been unable to contact the copyright holder of the cover of the *Popular Electronics*
magazine shown on page 22 and would be grateful for any information.

JB GAT

Published in Great Britain in 1994
by Exley Publications Ltd,
16 Chalk Hill, Watford,
Herts WD1 4BN, United Kingdom.

Copyright © Exley Publications, 1994
Copyright © David Marshall, 1994

**A copy of the CIP data is available from the
British Library on request.**

ISBN 1-85015-483-X

Editor: Samantha Armstrong
Editorial assistant: Helen Lanz
Picture editors: Alex Goldberg and James Clift
of Image Select
Typeset by Delta Print, Watford, Herts, U.K.
Printed in Hungary, 1994

BILL GATES

AND

MICROSOFT

DAVID MARSHALL

⩗EXLEY

Microsoft on every computer?

Bill Gates had a vision, "A computer on every desk, and in every home," and "Microsoft on every computer" was his dream.

In 1975, Bill Gates, aged nineteen, and his friend, Paul Allen, founded the computer software company Microsoft. Today, there are few, if any, major industries and commercial organizations that do not rely to some degree on computers. Computer skills have become necessary in almost all jobs and Bill Gates and Paul Allen had the vision to realize that this would happen.

"The electronic revolution has arrived, full force. And with it has come vast changes in how we work, how we play, how we interact, and even how we think." What Bill Gates did not add when he said this was that he, and his company, had been instrumental in creating that revolution!

"I wanted to write computer software, which is a very specialized thing. I knew it was going to be a big industry. I didn't know whether I would succeed or not, but I had this vision that computers would be valuable tools on every desk and, eventually, in every home."

Bill Gates, 1993.

Too much success?

In achieving his aim, Microsoft, after just fourteen years, became the first software company to sell more than a billion dollars' worth of products in one year.

Bill Gates himself, at thirty-one, was the youngest billionaire in American history. By 1991, he was worth more than $4 billion (over £2 billion) and he was fast becoming the richest person in the United States. The real testament to Bill Gates's success, however, was the move by other computer companies to try to break up Microsoft's huge business.

For some time, Microsoft's rivals had complained about the company's business practices. By 1990, these complaints had reached the Federal Trade Commission (FTC). The FTC is a United States government agency, made up of business lawyers, that looks into claims that companies are competing unfairly and are therefore threatening the welfare of other businesses.

One rival computer firm felt that Bill Gates had "kind of won fair and square," but that there was not much business left over for any other company. It was the "kind of" that led to the FTC investigations. Many people have doubts that any one company can be so successful without bending or breaking the rules. However, that same rival went on to give a clue to another possible explanation for Gates's success, "It's frightening to be up against him. While I'd prefer he not be in quite so much control of the world, I think that he has earned it."

Vision

In 1993, Bill Gates looked at how Microsoft could develop its future: "As we explore these new directions, we hope to put the raw power of computers to work in new ways, fundamentally improving how technology can serve our customers in their businesses and homes." The essence of Microsoft was to keep on top of developments in technology – often before they were even fully developed – and to sell them to its loyal customers.

When Bill Gates made his forecast about a computer on every desk, the personal computer did not even exist. Nevertheless, Gates had already realized that computers had "raw power." He knew that technology could serve customers both in the office and in the home. Bill Gates also knew how to make a deal.

He applied all of this knowledge with enthusiasm and drive. The word "workaholic" could have been coined to describe Bill Gates. He appeared to ignore his personal life and did not seem to care what he looked like to other people. He was not interested in the trappings of success – in expensive clothes or luxury apartments, for example – but found more pleasure in making deals. His wealth, he said, simply meant that he no longer had to worry about what he ordered in a restaurant. Despite the fact that he flew all over the world, he never went first class, always economy. In fact, besides work, his greatest passion was for fast cars – particularly Porsches.

But what was it about Bill Gates that made Microsoft so successful? Why did Microsoft send tremors through the world of computing?

Bill Gates in 1992, at the age of thirty-six. Microsoft got to the top of the pile in the computing industry, but customers did have problems with Microsoft products. However, rather than just listening and correcting, Microsoft made a policy of building those concerns into its future planning so that the same problems did not arise for other customers.

Above: An early calculating machine built between 1837 and 1843.
Left and right: In 1801, the revolutionary Jacquard loom used a series of punched cards to "tell" the machine what patterns to create – computers are "told" in a similar way today.

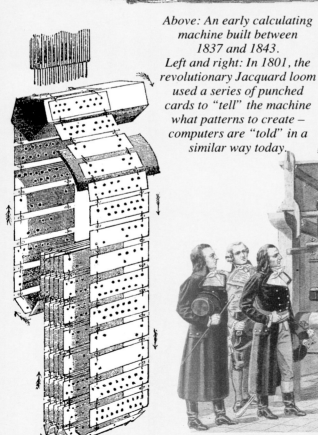

Above: Charles Babbage (1791-1871), inventor, mathematician, and philosopher, invented an "analytical engine" and a "difference machine." He is generally recognized as the grandfather of computing.

Left: Babbage's "difference machine" or mechanical computer – the world's first attempt to build a machine that could calculate and print out results. Financial constraints meant that it was never finished.

Computers, computers, computers

Today it seems obvious to most people that there is a way of telling a computer what to do through what is called a computer language. In the mid-seventies, nothing to do with personal computers was obvious. Much of the development in computers was a result of the vision and drive of particular, gifted people about two hundred years ago.

It all started in 1742, with a French mathematician, Blaise Pascal, who invented an adding machine. This was refined and developed in the mid-nineteenth century by Charles Babbage who, in 1823 developed a huge "analytical engine" that could actually be "programmed." Babbage is credited with being the "grandfather" of computers, yet it was over one hundred years later, in 1948, that the first real computer was built.

It wasn't until 1975 that the first personal, desktop computer, the Altair, was developed for use in the home and the office. The computer language that

told the Altair what to do was written by two young visionaries who were about to change the face of the personal computer business – Bill Gates and Paul Allen.

The computer language they developed was a type of language named BASIC – Beginners All-Purpose Symbolic Instruction Code. Different languages enable computers to perform different tasks. Bill Gates and Paul Allen wanted to use languages to turn computers on for the millions of potential customers who were, as yet, unaware of the difference computers were about to make in their lives.

William H. Gates III

William H. Gates was born on October 28, 1955 in Seattle, on the west coast of the United States. He was born into a wealthy family but never used its money in his own business. His mother, Mary, was a teacher and an important society figure in Seattle. Mary kept Bill organized. His father, known as Bill Jr., was an influential attorney who was strict but supportive with Bill and his sisters, Kristi and Libby.

As a child – and as an adult as well – Bill was untidy. It has been said that in order to counteract this, Mary drew up weekly clothing plans for him. On Mondays he might go to school in blue, on Tuesdays in green, on Wednesdays in brown, Thursdays in black, and so on. Weekend meal schedules might also be planned in detail. Everything had to fit in. Bill Gates hated wasting time, at work or during his leisure time.

Dinner table discussions in the Gates's family home were always lively and educational. "It was a rich environment in which to learn," Bill remembered.

The Sermon on the Mount

As a boy Bill seemed fairly ordinary – but in some respects he was very different. When he was eleven Bill attended religious confirmation classes where, as a challenge, Reverend Turner invited his students to

memorize chapters five, six, and seven of the Gospel of St. Matthew – better known as The Sermon on the Mount from the Bible. The prize was dinner at the top of Space Needle, one of the tallest buildings in Seattle.

The Sermon on the Mount is a difficult passage to learn because it is disjointed and repetitive – it is also very long. When Reverend Turner went to the Gates's home to listen to Bill, he was shocked. No one had ever been able to get through the passage without some prompting and many stumbles. Bill Gates simply began at the beginning and recited the whole thing without a moment's hesitation or a single mistake. When Reverend Turner expressed his amazement he was told, "I can do anything I put my mind to" by Bill.

This was not a boast – just a statement of fact that Bill Gates was later to prove to be all too true.

Above: Bill won a meal in the restaurant at the top of Space Needle overlooking Seattle, the city where he later based his business.

Opposite top and below: Bill Gates at three with his mother, Mary, and then at seven when he was in the eighth grade at Lakeside School. He was already an exceptional student.

A competitive nature

Bill's contemporaries, even at that age, recognized that he was exceptional. Every year, he and his friends would go to summer camp. Bill especially liked the sports and swimming. One of his summer camp friends recalled, "He was never a nerd or a goof or the kind of kid you didn't want on your team. We all knew Bill was smarter than us. Even back then, when he was nine or ten years old, he talked like an adult and could express himself in ways that none of us understood."

Bill was also well ahead of his classmates in mathematics and science. He needed to go to a school that challenged him. His parents decided to send him to Lakeside – an all-boys' school for exceptional students. It was Seattle's most exclusive school and was noted for its rigorous academic demands, a place where "even the dumb kids were smart."

Lakeside allowed students to pursue their own interests, to whatever extent they wished. The school prided itself on making conditions and facilities available that would enable all its students to reach their full potential. It was the ideal environment for someone like Bill Gates.

In 1968, the school made a decision that would change thirteen year old Bill Gates's life – and that of many others, too.

Computer access

Funds were raised, mainly by parents, that enabled the school to gain access to a computer – a Program Data Processor (PDP) – through a teletype machine. Type in a few instructions on the teletype machine and a few seconds later the PDP would type back its response. Bill Gates was immediately hooked – so was his best friend at the time, Kent Evans, and another student, Paul Allen, who was two years older than Bill.

Whenever they had free time, and sometimes when they didn't, they would dash over to the computer room to use the machine. The students became so single-minded that they soon overtook

Bill Gates and Paul Allen using the teletype machine at Lakeside School in 1970. Gates was just fifteen years old but looked much younger, and Allen was seventeen. Just five years after this photograph was taken the two friends decided to form Microsoft and "make some real money."

their teachers in knowledge about computing and got into a lot of trouble because of their obsession. They were neglecting their other studies – every piece of work was handed in late. Classes were cut. Computer time was also proving to be very expensive. Within months, the whole budget that had been set aside for the year had been used up.

Lakeside School in Seattle. When Bill Gates attended it was an all-boys' school, though now it is coeducational. Its academic standards challenged Bill and he later donated money for a new mathematics and science building for the school.

BASIC and business magazines

At fourteen, Bill was already writing short programs for the computer to perform. Early games programs such as Tic-Tac-Toe, or Noughts and Crosses, and Lunar Landing were written in what was to become Bill's second language, BASIC.

One of the reasons Bill was so good at programming is because it is mathematical and logical. During his time at Lakeside, Bill scored a perfect eight hundred on a mathematics test. It was extremely important to him to get this grade – he had to take the test more than once in order to do it.

Opposite top: This picture
of Bill Gates in the
computer room at Lakeside
was taken in 1973.

Opposite below:
Lakeside's computer room
in 1993 – a far cry from
the single teletype machine
of just twenty-three
years earlier.

If Bill Gates was going to be good at something, it was essential to be the best.

Bill's and Paul's fascination with computers and the business world meant that they read a great deal. Paul enjoyed magazines like *Popular Electronics*, while Bill read business magazines. Computer time was expensive and, because both boys were desperate to get more time and because Bill already had an insight into what they could achieve financially, the two of them decided to set themselves up as a company: The Lakeside Programmers Group. "Let's call the real world and try to sell something to it!" Bill announced.

First venture

A local computer firm in Seattle, Computer Center Corporation, or C-Cubed as Bill and Paul nicknamed it, heard about how the Lakeside students had become obsessed with their computer and offered to make a deal with the school for access to its PDP too.

It was the best idea C-Cubed could have had and the students became even more obsessed, using all sorts of programs as well as crashing – that is, bringing down the system – many times. They also ran up huge bills almost immediately. Once, Bill and a couple of his friends broke the computer's security system and found C-Cubed's accounting system. They also found the Lakeside account and reduced the figure they owed! Unfortunately for Bill, the company picked up the changes, called the school, and Bill was given a six-week ban from the computer.

But Bill Gates returned with even greater energy. Because of their enthusiasm, the boys of The Lakeside Programmers Group were crashing the system, making it completely unusable, with increasing regularity. Unfortunately when they crashed the system they not only stopped themselves from pursuing their own interests but they also stopped all of C-Cubed's paying customers.

C-Cubed came up with a novel solution to its problem. It gave the students free computer time in order to find faults or bugs in its software. Computer

Bugs in a computer are a well known irritation to all users. They are called bugs because, in 1945, an early computer at Harvard University, in the United States, failed. An assistant searched through the numerous cables and wires and found a large moth had landed in the workings. The first computer bug was removed with a pair of tweezers!

software is the overall term for three different elements: the operating system, languages, and applications. The operating system controls the basic functions of the computer, enabling the computer to work, the languages enable the user to give instructions and applications are the computer programs themselves.

The students worked the night shift so that they were not using the computer during the busy office hours. All they had to do to get unlimited access to the computer was to make an accurate record of how and where they found any bugs. They would stay up all night, exist on a diet of Coke and pizza, and then go to school the next day.

Bill Gates's and Paul Allen's devotion and unconventional life style had begun. But, like many successful business people, they needed a stroke of luck to really get underway as a business – followed by tremendous dedication.

A year off

At the age of fourteen, Bill was spending nights and days on end at the computer. His parents insisted on him taking some time off. Bill agreed to avoid the computer room for almost a year to catch up with his studies. "I tried to be normal," he remembered. He worked hard and caught up. When the year was over Bill simply went back to the routine as before.

Despite the year off, Bill was a computer guru to the other students at Lakeside. He stood out. If anyone at Lakeside was asked who was the real genius among geniuses, Bill Gates was the answer.

Despite all The Lakeside Programmers Group's work, C-Cubed's computer continued to be riddled with faults. It would have taken more than seven years to clear the software of all the bugs – and by that time the company would have gone out of business.

The first deal

In 1970 C-Cubed failed and Bill Gates made the first of many good deals and showed how ruthless he could be.

Without telling Paul Allen and the others, he and his friend, Kent bought, and hid, C-Cubed's valuable computer tapes. When Paul discovered this, he took the tapes. Bill threatened to sue him if they were not returned. So Paul returned them. A little while later Bill sold the tapes at a profit. Bill had shown that he could cut a deal and beat off any threat to his interests.

At fourteen, Bill Gates knew he would be a millionaire by the time he was thirty. He already had a good idea of how to do business, and he and Paul Allen had a vision of the world with a computer on every desk.

Opposite: Bill Gates looking relaxed and sitting still. Both Bill Gates and Paul Allen were eager to get involved in the new area of personal computers. Gates's vision was to get software working for people rather than computers, and for people to find using a computer as much fun as he did – like going to the movies or calling a friend.

A payroll program – Bill Gates takes over

In 1971, The Lakeside Programmers Group got its first real business opportunity – although it didn't make any money from it. It was asked to write a payroll program for a local company, Information Sciences, Inc. (ISI). Bill was excluded at first as there wasn't enough work for the whole group.

The problems of road congestion and air pollution are a direct result of the increasing number of vehicles on the roads. Most cities use a counting system to monitor the traffic. In the 1970s, this was a slow and laborious process. Gates and Allen chose this problem for their first computer project. With their Traf-O-Data program, developed when Bill was about sixteen, they attempted to get a computer to analyze all the traffic information.

The others, however, found it difficult to make any real progress and eventually had to ask Bill to join them. He took charge and the program was delivered on time. Although ISI had signed a royalties deal with the students, it actually "paid" The Lakeside Programmers Group in free computer time. They, and Bill in particular, had learned a lot more about making deals. Because it was a real business deal, The Lakeside Programmers Group had to become a formal company. Bill's father, Bill Gates Jr., helped with the legal formalities. He became its principal legal adviser. At the time Bill Gates and Kent Evans were fifteen years old.

"If anybody wants to know why Bill Gates is where he is today, in my judgment it's because of this early experience in cutting deals," recalled Kent's father.

Traf-O-Data

In order to get involved in more deals, Gates and Allen came up with the idea of a system to ease the traffic flow in cities – Traf-O-Data. Almost all towns and cities analyzed traffic flow by using a system of rubber hoses placed across roads and connected to boxes containing paper tape that was punched every time a vehicle went over the hose.

Gates and Allen devised a computer program that analyzed the markings on the paper quicker than the usual team of human analysts – and more efficiently. They also thought that they could do the job even more effectively if they had their own computer. So they built one.

It was a great idea, but the computer was never particularly reliable and the desire to build their own computer did not become a driving ambition. It was always important to control the computers they had access to, but Gates and Allen were prepared to let others build the machines. They simply wanted to provide the means to make them work. At this early stage, Bill Gates and Paul Allen were only interested in languages.

The Logic Simulation Company

Gates was ambitious to make even better deals, and real money, even though he was still going to school. He formed a different computer group with Kent Evans named the Logic Simulation Company. In order to expand, they invited other students to join them. They made it clear that they did not just want to recruit "computer freaks" and that there would be "equal opportunity for males and females." Gates and Evans just wanted the best.

In May 1972, the school board asked Gates and Evans to computerize their school's class schedule. Just a week later, Kent Evans was killed in a mountain climbing accident. Despite this shock, Paul Allen joined Bill Gates to do the work and Lakeside School still uses a form of their program for its scheduling.

At the age of seventeen, it was expected that Gates would go to the oldest and most prestigious university in the United States, Harvard, and graduate top of his class. Well, he went to Harvard and at least began the process.

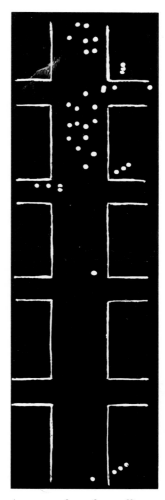

A screen shot of a traffic simulation computer program. The dots on the road represent traffic – cars, small trucks and large trucks. The triple dots are traffic lights. Analysts use computer images like this to ease traffic flow. Traf-O-Data successfully produced charts of the traffic flow in Seattle.

Harvard

At Harvard, Bill Gates found he was not the best at mathematics. As far as the future was concerned, his intention had always been to become a mathematician. But he discovered that he was not going to be the very best mathematician. If he couldn't be the best, then why bother?

He became known for working at only those problems that challenged him and always being able to find the solutions. He also became obsessed with winning at cards. When he wasn't playing cards he could be found at a computer. His sleep and work patterns became even more bizarre than when he had been working nights on C-Cubed's computer – work for thirty-six hours, sleep for ten, and then start again, even if it was 4:00 A.M. The computer room was often empty at night – except for Gates. When

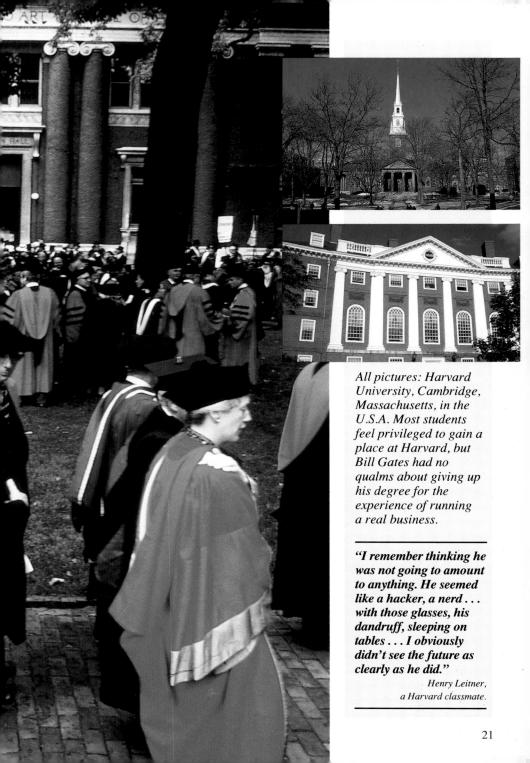

All pictures: Harvard University, Cambridge, Massachusetts, in the U.S.A. Most students feel privileged to gain a place at Harvard, but Bill Gates had no qualms about giving up his degree for the experience of running a real business.

"I remember thinking he was not going to amount to anything. He seemed like a hacker, a nerd ... with those glasses, his dandruff, sleeping on tables ... I obviously didn't see the future as clearly as he did."

Henry Leitner,
a Harvard classmate.

The magazine cover that led to a computer software revolution and the formation of Microsoft. Popular Electronics announced the first minicomputer kit – the Altair 8800. It had no screen or keyboard and was fed information through a tape machine; otherwise it was programmed using the switches on the front in hundreds of different combinations. Until Gates and Allen stepped in the Altair could not do anything – their version of the computer language BASIC made it work.

he became totally exhausted he would often go to sleep on the tables, only to be woken up by the first class in the morning. He had all the hallmarks of a classic "computer nerd" – excessively bright, fixated on computers, adept at "hacking" (which means using the computer simply for entertainment and also accessing computers without permission), irregular personal habits, not to mention wearing glasses.

One day, another student found Bill Gates filling in a tax return. It was a declaration of the money he had earned from the Traf-O-Data business. None of the other students had even the remotest idea of how to fill in such a form – but Bill Gates already knew.

One student, Steve Ballmer, was impressed by Gates's intensity and knowledge and he lived just down the hall for most of the first year. He, too, was able to go without sleep in the same way that Gates could, and he also got very wound up when arguing a point. Steve Ballmer was to be important to Bill Gates a few years later when Bill was looking for a kindred spirit to join Microsoft.

The Microsoft revolution

If there was one moment that began the Microsoft revolution it was on a particularly cold December day in 1974 when Paul Allen was crossing Harvard Square to visit Bill Gates.

He happened to notice the latest copy of the magazine, *Popular Electronics*. On the cover there was a picture of the Altair 8800 – a personal computer that was to be sold as a kit, in direct competition with commercial computers. Allen could see that this could mean the beginning of personal computers being available to everyone and anyone. He dashed off to see Gates, who was then just nineteen years old, and said, "Well, here's our opportunity to do something with BASIC."

Both Gates and Allen realized that the personal computer revolution was about to happen. Gates also anticipated the deals that were to be made if they could get involved in providing the software for these new computers.

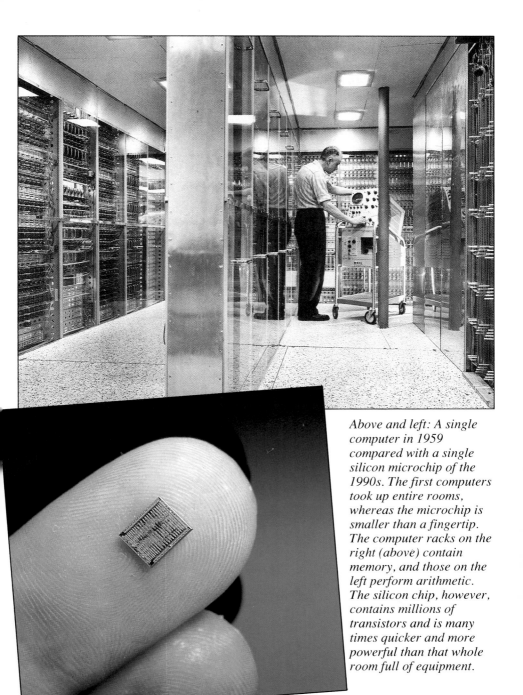

Above and left: A single computer in 1959 compared with a single silicon microchip of the 1990s. The first computers took up entire rooms, whereas the microchip is smaller than a fingertip. The computer racks on the right (above) contain memory, and those on the left perform arithmetic. The silicon chip, however, contains millions of transistors and is many times quicker and more powerful than that whole room full of equipment.

BASIC

The company that made the Altair computer was Model Instrumentation and Telemetry Systems (MITS). The owner of MITS, Ed Roberts, needed a simple computer language for the Altair. The most simple language was BASIC and, along with many others, Gates and Allen told Roberts that they could provide a version of BASIC for the Altair. Gates and Allen knew that they needed a routine that would make the computer do simple basic arithmetical processes. No one had ever written a BASIC for a personal computer before.

Roberts was rather disbelieving about all the claims. However, despite not even having the computer, Gates and Allen got to work developing BASIC for the Altair 8800 personal computer.

They worked day and night for eight weeks to complete it. They had to work with a diagram of the Altair from *Popular Electronics* and the computer's manual because they didn't have the Altair itself. Their grasp of this new technology was incredible.

In fact, when Allen went to deliver the BASIC program to Ed Roberts, it suddenly occurred to him in one horrifying moment that they had not written a loader program or a routine that would enable the Altair to actually receive their BASIC program before running it. Allen wrote it – out of his head in complicated computer language – straight onto a piece of paper. Later, when he fed the tape on which the program was written into a tape reader attached to the Altair, it worked perfectly. So did their BASIC, and Gates and Allen were on their way.

"I was dazzled," Roberts remembered. "It was certainly impressive … I was very impressed that we got anywhere near as far as we did that day."

Microsoft is born

The Altair, with its working BASIC, was an amazing breakthrough in computer terms. It was also the single event that caused Microsoft – derived from the words microcomputer software – to be born.

In 1975, Gates and Allen, as Microsoft, officially

signed a deal for their BASIC with MITS. The company goal at that time was to provide languages for the Altair and all the other personal computers that would surely follow on to the market. It was the first company specifically formed for this purpose.

Gates, still only nineteen years old, not only understood the complex technology better than almost anyone else, he also had a grasp of the novel legal issues involved in licensing their software. He made sure that the licensing of their BASIC did not depend on the sale of MITS hardware. He granted MITS the right to use and market the Microsoft BASIC but did not sell it to them outright. Microsoft kept the ownership of the program regardless of who used or distributed it. In this, Bill Gates set a standard for future software deals.

The designer of the Altair 8800 and owner of MITS, Ed Roberts. A gifted man who, through the stress of the job, eventually gave it up and qualified as a doctor. He was impressed with Gates's and Allen's drive and insight and predicted that they would become millionaires if "they didn't die first!"

The personal computer boom begins

Almost from the moment they met him, Bill Gates and Paul Allen did not get along with Ed Roberts. Over the years, they were to have many differences of opinion with Roberts over how to do business, but

Allen still went to Albuquerque in New Mexico and was employed as MITS's software director. In reality, he was the only software writer there.

The staff at MITS was working all hours to keep up with the phenomenal demand for the first personal computer, the Altair. The *Popular Electronics* article had sparked a public response that was hard to cope with. It had promised delivery of the Altair computer kit to everyone who applied – and within two months. Roberts also demanded their BASIC on a diskette – a forerunner of the floppy disk – from Gates and Allen and they provided it in less than two weeks. Programs stored on the disk could be loaded onto the computer.

It was all coming together for Gates and Allen – their unsocial hours, complete dedication, and tremendous ability had set them on their way.

Copying

Gates soon saw that computer fanatics were imitating their version of BASIC. He wrote angry letters to computer and electronic's magazines. He accused amateurs of stealing. He became well known, but not for the reasons he would have liked. When he was interviewed as a result of the protest he was making, Bill said he was angry at his company not getting what it deserved from the work it had done. He was only twenty, looked fourteen, but still commanded respect.

This was Gates's first real insight into the copying problem that has plagued the software industry. He made the point that if copying persisted, the money that people like themselves needed to develop new products would simply not be forthcoming – so neither would new software.

Microsoft's first offices

Gates and Allen now began to assemble a group of gifted programmers around them in their new company. They were located in Albuquerque as Allen was still working for MITS and Bill was officially still at Harvard. These unconventional,

". . . Gates demonstrated a combination of talents that is rare among inventor-entrepreneurs. Besides processing technical skills and expertise, he has also displayed an impressive flair for business."

From Scanorama, *September 1993.*

high-IQ, insomniacs became known as the Microkids. Marc McDonald, a twenty-one year old, who arrived in Albuquerque in April 1976, was from the Lakeside School computer room. He took on the task of providing a version of BASIC for the filing system of the National Cash Register Company – one of the two big customers gained by Gates and Allen in late 1976. General Electric was the other.

Soon Allen gave up his job with MITS to work full-time for Microsoft. It now looked likely that its first year's income would be over $100,000 (£55,000), and they expected to triple it the following year. Two eminent programmers, Albert Chu and Steve Woods, both just twenty-four, arrived to work on a development of the language FORTRAN (Formula Translation), which, as far as Gates and Allen were concerned, was the next direction for languages.

As a result of this expansion, Microsoft opened its first offices – consisting of four rooms on the eighth floor of a bank building near Albuquerque airport.

One of the Microsoft employees in the Seattle-based offices. The same philosophy of a relaxed atmosphere with a casual dress code was adopted in the very first office in Albuquerque. Bill Gates himself was always more interested in the work he was doing than in the way he looked or keeping strict office hours. This flexibility enabled Microsoft employees to give their best work hours to the company – day or night.

A dropout?

In January 1977, Bill Gates dropped out of Harvard University – permanently. His parents were extremely alarmed – they were not sure whether he had a real grasp of what he was attempting. After all, no one had been a computer tycoon yet. In fact, most people had never used or even seen a personal computer.

The university itself did not acknowledge that he had left for good. It was inconceivable to them that anyone would not want the inspiration and insurance that a Harvard degree would give to an aspiring business executive. Gates seems not to have needed the comfort or confidence that Harvard could supply.

He dropped out partly because he had become bored with the people, partly because most of the work didn't interest him, and mainly because Microsoft was taking off and he needed to be there. For the next five years, Gates would devote himself exclusively to building the business. Except for two short breaks he was rarely away from Microsoft – night or day.

Do not underestimate Bill Gates

One of the first things Gates wanted to do was cancel the agreement with Ed Roberts and MITS. Roberts had said that he would never block a deal Microsoft made to sell its BASIC – unless it was to a competitor of the Altair – and that he would make his "best effort" to line up other deals for Microsoft's programs. In 1975 that had not been a problem because there were no other personal computers.

However, by 1977, Commodore had brought out its PET, Tandy was perfecting its TRS-80, and Apple was emerging with its Apple II. All these hardware manufacturers would need to acquire a version of BASIC – and Microsoft could supply it. It would have to break with MITS to make real money.

Things came to a head when Roberts sold MITS to another company named Pertec. By this time the Altair was selling in very small numbers. The only real asset MITS had was BASIC – and Bill Gates and Microsoft wanted that back.

When Pertec's lawyers met Gates they relied on their first impression – a twenty-one year old who looked much younger. In addition to underestimating him, Pertec wrote a letter to Microsoft saying that it would no longer market BASIC or allow it to be licensed because it considered every other hardware company a competitor. This went completely against the "best efforts" clause in Microsoft's agreement with MITS, and Bill Gates immediately picked Pertec up on this. As Microsoft's Steve Woods observed, "They came in very arrogant, essentially saying, 'We are this huge multimillion dollar company and you are just a handful of kids and we are not going to take you seriously.' And that was a big mistake."

"We set the standard"

Thanks to the court ruling that Microsoft owned the rights to its BASIC, Bill Gates was now free to sell BASIC wherever and whenever he wanted. His natural business sense and foresight had paid off once again.

The money started to flow in like water as

It takes courage – some would say foolhardiness – to drop out of Harvard and go into the business world without any formal qualifications. To Bill Gates it seemed the sensible thing to do. Harvard was getting in the way of making deals and spreading the influence of the newly-formed Microsoft. He reasoned that there was nothing Harvard could teach him that he needed to know. Events proved him right, but this may not be true for many people!

Opposite: "Children can be the best critics, because they respond directly. They'll tell us what's hot and what's not, without us needing to probe very much!" Microsoft's general manager revealed. "Our hope is to create a new generation of software that is in touch with this generation of kids, preparing them for tomorrow while making their learning experiences richer today."

Microsoft sold its BASIC to Commodore, Apple, Radio Shack, NCR, General Electric, Texas Instruments, Intel, and others. "Just a plain version of Disk BASIC went for $50,000 (£29,000), and we could make the thing in a couple of hours," one of the programmers recalled.

Microsoft could – but hardly any other company at that time had that capacity or knowledge. Certainly no one else had its drive to succeed. For the first time, Microsoft was beginning to be the standard for the whole computer industry. Gates said, "We set the standard" – and he meant it.

More contracts

While Allen and the other programmers concentrated on pushing the software industry forward, Gates pursued deals with other businesses. He went after original equipment manufacturers – companies making products that needed a computer in order for them to function.

Inside every computer-controlled machine – washing machine, car assembly line, telephone exchange, cash register till – there has to be some sort of computer. Inside every computer there has to be an operating system and a language. As far as Gates was concerned Microsoft had to sell to all these manufacturers – and it usually did.

He also decided to go for the Japanese market and in this respect, too, he was well ahead of everyone else. He could see that Japan was going to be the major place for computer development. He hooked up with another computer whiz kid with whom he had a lot in common, Kuzuhiko Nishi. They were more or less the same age, both were brilliant, both came from well-to-do backgrounds, both knew instinctively how to make deals, both had dropped out of college to form their own companies, and both were to become millionaires.

Nishi formed the ASCII publishing company which became the largest software company in Japan. He became Gates's eyes and ears in Japan. The one-page agreement they signed in 1977 produced millions of dollars for both Nishi and Microsoft.

The Microkids in 1978.
Microsoft had fewer
than a dozen employees
when this photograph
was taken; in 1994 it
had operations in forty-
one countries with over
fourteen thousand
employees. Bill Gates is
in the bottom row, far
left and Paul Allen is in
the same row, far right.

Work hard, make better products, and win

Now there was no holding Microsoft back. Its growth was nothing short of fabulous. All who worked there had a common ideal – work hard, make better products, and win. It was now based in a suite of five offices in Albuquerque with a staff of six members. The office doors were all left open and the programmers worked as many hours as necessary to do the job. They typed into computers all day, printing out reams of paper. The pace was frenetic. Gates worked seven-day weeks and often slept on the office floor. The employees extended their hours – none of them wanting to be the first to leave. The atmosphere encouraged a relaxed but committed work ethic. No one wore suits, just jeans and T-shirts, and free soft drinks were provided. Soon, in order to keep a balance in its office affairs and to take care of the administration of the business, a secretary joined the company.

Miriam Lubow was appointed when Gates was away on a business trip. When he got back, she protested that "some kid had gone into Mr. Gates's office and was messing with the equipment." It was gently pointed out to her that the "kid" was Gates himself.

On finding out that his wife's new boss was a twenty-one year old, Miriam's husband suggested she make sure she was paid at the end of the month! She would later become something of a surrogate mother to Gates.

At the end of 1978, Gates and Allen decided that they had to move: Microsoft needed bigger premises because business had boomed. The reason for this success was twofold. First, the Microkids were almost fanatical in the way they worked because of their profound desire to work on computers and the fact that they were pushed hard at all times. It was impossible for them not to work tremendously long hours, because Gates himself did. He never expected anyone to do more than he did but, he did not expect that they would do any less.

Passionate belief

Gates was, and continued to be, the best sort of business executive. He knew and believed passionately in his product. He believed that it was better to get any deal than no deal at all. He was tireless and worked all hours. He ignored tradition. Because of his zeal and knowledge, his staff always went with him. If he could eat cold pizza and work all night without thinking about it, so could his workforce – and it did!

Also, the whole personal computer business was going crazy. It seemed no one could get a computer out fast enough to satisfy consumer demand – and all the computers needed something from Microsoft inside them. By this time, the number of employees was up to thirteen and Microsoft had made its first million. In order to expand easily and to be closer to Gates's and Allen's families Microsoft chose to leave Albuquerque and go back to Seattle. Most of the staff loyally chose to go with it.

"Just thinking of things as winning is a terrible approach. Success comes from focusing in on what you really like and are good at – not challenging every random thing."
Bill Gates, from the New Yorker,
Jan. 10, 1994.

Staff management

The early development of Microsoft was fraught with problems over the way Gates, still just in his early twenties, handled the rest of the staff. With a short temper, and an impatient, and confrontational manner, people found him difficult to work with. His mannerism of rocking backwards and forwards in meetings revealed his intensity. He was, and continued to be, very hard to satisfy. If groups of programmers worked on a project for weeks, it would not be unusual for Gates simply to say that the result was poor and that they needed to do it again. He always drove those around him at a frantic pace – and screamed at them if he felt they had not given their best to Microsoft.

The computer is the most important machine in modern business life. Basic office tasks involve the production, storage, and relay of information. Microsoft saw the potential of the market and focused its product development appropriately.

When the company moved to Seattle in January 1979, Miriam Lubow was replaced by Marla Woods. At first, Marla was the only member of the office staff. She acted as receptionist, performed all clerical duties, got hamburgers and milk shakes for the programmers, and worked the same hours as the rest of them.

Gradually, as the company grew, more secretaries were taken on. To Gates, the administrative employees had no technical expertise and, as he had been used to doing all the office work himself for years, he underestimated and undervalued their contribution to the company.

The administrative staff members wanted to be paid for all the overtime they were putting in – with back pay. Marla Wood went to her boss to put in the claim. Her boss was also her husband, Steve Wood. He took the claim to Gates, who refused to consider it. Marla and the rest of the administrative staff threatened to take their claim to the state Department of Labor and Industries. Gates thought they were bluffing and told them to try it.

They did, and Gates was furious, believing that they were trying to ruin his business. After a short time they heard that they had won their claim and were paid for their overtime. The amount of money involved was just a few hundred dollars – the amount of bitterness caused was huge.

Gates learned from the experience. He brought in his old friend from Harvard, Steve Ballmer, as assistant to the president. Ballmer was very similar to Gates in attitude and temperament. They would often argue and get impatient with each other, but the confrontations were always about what was best for the company. Ballmer became an integral part of the Microsoft success story and indispensable to Gates.

Top staff

The way that Microsoft recruited gave great insight into the intensity of the business and how important it is to get the right staff. Bill Gates believed that Microsoft's success would always be based on the company's ability to attract – and keep – qualified employees.

Almost from the moment he joined the company, Steve Ballmer was Microsoft's recruiting coordinator – although Gates would sometimes join in. A high IQ was always an essential for anyone joining the company. Almost always, Gates wanted young people straight out of college. Microsoft did not pay particularly well, but it was able to hire anyone by offering a thrusting environment in which to work, free membership to local health clubs, a relaxed, yet committed working atmosphere, and generous opportunities to buy into the stock of the company.

In order to succeed at Microsoft, a recruit had to have unlimited drive and enthusiasm. The company chose around twenty universities in the United States, Canada, and Japan as its prime targets and went for the most exceptional students. It made personal visits to the universities and held informal interviews. It asked difficult and bizarre questions to see how the students would react. It asked

Stock Options

If a company needs more capital, or basic reserves, it may decide to go public through a listing on the stock market or stock exchange. This means that people from outside the company are allowed to buy shares in that company.

Anyone who buys "shares" in a company becomes a part-owner of that company – and is called a "shareholder" or "stockholder."

It is only possible to buy shares in an incorporated, or public limited, company. These are firms whose ownership is divided up into millions of shares, which are listed on the stock market or stock exchange.

People buy shares to make money from a company's profits and from increases in the value of the business. Those profits that are shared out among the share/stockholders are paid out as dividends during the year. The dividends are higher when the company is making large profits and lower when profits are down. Higher dividends also raise the cash price of the individual shares, if they are sold.

Many companies nowadays run share/stock owning schemes for their work force, as offered by Microsoft. These are called Employee Share/Stock Option Schemes (ESOP). The thinking is that owning shares in the business gives workers a stake in the success of the company.

Shares in a private company, held in an ESOP trust, are given a cash value each year by the company's accountants. Worker-shareholders can then decide whether to hold on to their shares or sell them.

formidable technical questions and gave the interviewees pen and paper and asked them to solve them. If they solved the questions, rode through, or, better still, enjoyed the pressure of the interview and had the capacity to look beyond the obvious, then they fitted in at Microsoft.

Work hours at Microsoft were completely flexible. Writing programs is creative and intense work and people need to feel relaxed and self-motivated. Some people might choose to work a night shift – coming in at 10:00 P.M. and leaving at 6:00 A.M. To keep the team atmosphere that Gates and Allen started with, teams of between five and fifteen always worked on specific projects.

IBM enters the personal computer world

In July 1979, Microsoft hired its first marketing director, Steve Smith. He was thirty-four and looked the part; Bill Gates was now twenty-three, still looked seventeen, and until he began to speak, lacked credibility.

It was important, however, that Microsoft seemed credible when it was approached by the biggest computer company in the world – IBM. If IBM was to continue to dominate the computer industry it needed to develop a suitable personal computer, one that was small enough for use in the home and versatile enough for use in the office for administrative work.

Gates and Allen were approached to provide both an operating system and languages for IBM's personal computer. Microsoft was dealing almost exclusively with languages, like BASIC and FORTRAN. To take advantage of IBM's business proposal, it was going to have to look at developing operating systems as well.

Getting into operating systems

Anyone who needed a particular software application for their computer could get it based on the language that Microsoft had already written for that particular machine. But each machine could have any number

of operating systems and it was a great nuisance to Microsoft's programmers that there were so many operating systems in the new computers.

It meant that every time they sat down at a new machine they had to modify BASIC for the system it was going to run on. It would have been very helpful if all the machines had the same operating system.

To try to do this, whenever they were approached by a client interested in purchasing a computer set-up, they recommended that they get in touch with Gates's long-time friend from his C-Cubed days, Gary Kildall, and use his operating system. In return, Kildall would recommend Microsoft to his clients. It was not that each didn't want to try what the other was doing. There was just so much work around that there wasn't time to do it all. It was only when IBM was considering its move into personal computers that emotional differences between the two companies began to emerge.

IBM wanted to be at the leading edge of personal computing. It was investing millions of dollars in its new product and wanted it to be the best. It decided to go for the Microsoft BASIC language and all the applications that came with it. The Microsoft BASIC would work on the new IBM machines – but the COBOL, FORTRAN, and Pascal languages that IBM had requested from Microsoft would not. So, in September 1980, Gates told IBM to talk to Gary Kildall about his operating system and getting these other languages working on that. He even spoke to Gary Kildall to arrange the meeting. In the light of what happened later over MS-DOS, this was an amazing turn of events.

Turn of events

The chief negotiator from IBM, Jack Sams, later described the meeting with Kildall as a mess. When IBM representatives arrived to meet Gary Kildall he was not there. The secrecy surrounding the negotiations with IBM was so tight that Kildall didn't realize who he was supposed to be meeting.

So IBM was left without an operating system for its new computer. Gates was aware that problems had occurred and was becoming anxious over where this all-important IBM contract was going. He was appalled that the lack of an operating system – only a small amount of work – was jeopardizing a deal for them for all the languages. In a series of meetings IBM instructed Microsoft to get them an operating system quickly. It didn't need to be told twice!

MS-DOS

If Bill Gates, almost twenty-five, was lucky when the negotiations with Kildall collapsed, then he had incredible good fortune over the operating system. To develop the system from nothing would be a hugely expensive and time-consuming exercise, yet Gates, in his ambitious way, anticipated that it would take just a year to develop.

However, he heard that an operating system had already been developed by Tim Paterson at Seattle Computer Products. It was

A whole set of books can be slipped into a pocket if they are stored on floppy disks. When the disks were first used for storing information they were a fairly large ten inches (25cms) across – and they really were floppy. Today most disks for personal computers are only 3.5 inches (9cms) across and are not floppy at all.

a rough and ready system known as 86-QDOS – the Quick and Dirty Operating System. Microsoft needed this system desperately.

Under an agreement that Gates himself put together, Microsoft bought the right to use QDOS for just $25,000 (£13,000) – probably the greatest deal ever made in the short history of the computer industry. Microsoft then modified and improved it for IBM. It became MS-DOS – Microsoft Disk Operating System – and Microsoft's passport to the stars.

So, after two months of secret negotiations, Microsoft proposed that it could provide IBM with four high-level languages for its personal computer – BASIC, FORTRAN, COBOL, and Pascal, and its operating system.

The IBM deal is struck

On his way to IBM to finalize the deal, Gates realized he didn't have a tie with him. Rather than go to an IBM meeting without a tie, he stopped to buy one and arrived half an hour late. Better late than without a tie.

MS-DOS was licensed to IBM because it did not

Bill Gates holding a floppy disk with the latest version of MS-DOS on it. Thanks to Microsoft constantly improving its products and being ruthless in its marketing, a copy of MS-DOS sold every three seconds somewhere in the world in 1993, and a copy of WINDOWS every four seconds. If the thousands of Microsoft applications on the market were included, then it was likely that every second of every day someone bought a Microsoft product.

At Microsoft, it was the quality of the work and the product that mattered, not how neat the office was. People who looked at customers' needs and tried to solve them had to feel comfortable and relaxed to perform at their best.

have time to develop its own operating system. The deal was that whenever an IBM personal computer was sold, Microsoft got a royalty even if the computer did not have MS-DOS – or any of Microsoft's software on it. So IBM was obliged to always provide MS-DOS in its personal computers.

In the following years, IBM's products were cloned more than any other company's. Its personal computers set the industry standard for hardware – but because of its rush to get the computer onto the market, over 80% of the components were from other companies. This made it easier for other manufacturers to copy the computer and produce what are known as IBM compatibles.

IBM gained nothing from this mimicry – Microsoft did, because each clone had to have an

operating system – and therefore had to license MS-DOS. Before finalizing the deal with IBM, Gates had needed to own the exclusive rights to 86-QDOS from Seattle Computers. He was anxious to avoid being tied to IBM and not having the flexibility to approach others. After very little bargaining he was able to buy the complete rights to 86-QDOS for $50,000 (£22,000) – a bargain.

When IBM and Microsoft began their relationship in 1980 they were at opposite ends of the business spectrum: IBM had 340,000 employees and $3.6 billion (£1.5 billion) annual earnings; Microsoft was still only a start-up company with around thirty-two employees and a fairly slim profit margin. But Microsoft had Bill Gates and, thanks to him, it also had MS-DOS.

Applications take off

Applications are programs that allow a computer to perform specific functions. For instance, they turn a computer into a word processor, or machine that can be used like a typewriter but which stores information as well. Bill Gates visualized another huge market – and fortune – in applications software. This was to be the third string – along with BASIC and the other languages and the MS-DOS operating system – to Microsoft's business.

In 1981 Gates decided to get Microsoft heavily involved in the applications market. He wanted to write and market the best word processor program, the best accounts program, the best program for information, or database. Microsoft was slow to get started in this area – but once underway it was ruthless. Gates could see that, although it was being extremely successful in certain areas, it needed to continue its expansion into other areas in order to secure its place in the market.

In 1982, Ballmer persuaded Gates that they needed a professional manager. None of the work force had ever had any management training. James Towne from Tektronix was appointed. It was a significant appointment mainly because it was so inappropriate. Towne was an excellent manager but just did not know how to cope with Microsoft's unconventional work ethos of working all hours and living, eating, and sleeping Microsoft. After eleven months Gates had to "let him go."

Gates admitted that hiring Towne was a mistake. As a manager he learned from his mistakes.

Paul Allen leaves

Late in 1982 Paul Allen became seriously unwell. After tests, Hodgkin's disease (cancer of the lymph nodes) was diagnosed. After eight years of tough eighty-hour weeks and few, if any, breaks, Allen withdrew partially from Microsoft. In 1983 he decided to withdraw completely from the company. After some time, the disease went into remission.

Although he was less visible than Gates, it was

Paul Allen and Bill Gates, the co-founders of Microsoft – one read electronic and technical magazines, the other business and management publications. One had wide interests, while the other was more focused. They both had great drive and energy – together they seemed unstoppable.

also due to Paul Allen's dedication and vision in the creation of Microsoft that the company came to fruition.

Microsoft Word

Competition in the applications market was hotting up. Another software company, Lotus, had launched an accounting program in direct competition to Microsoft's and this had hurt Gates.

Lotus had taken a gamble that the IBM personal computer would be the standard machine and that everyone would have one. So it made its accounting program fit the IBM personal computer. It would not run on any other machine. But, because it was just for this one machine, it was incredibly slick and fast. Microsoft's was written to work on many other machines, so it was slower. Lotus's risk paid off. It showed how important it is to be in the marketplace with a good product, and as quickly as possible – this was normally an essential part of Gates's marketing strategy.

". . . sometimes customers do express dissatisfaction with one aspect or another of our products or our business, and yes, we hear them and we follow up on their concerns. What's even more important is that we build that knowledge into our operations and planning, reshaping how we do business so those concerns won't arise with other customers in the future."
Bill Gates, 1993.

A computer room with desktop personal computers, a fax-modem, a laser printer, a super touch screen, a CD-ROM drive, a file-server, mouse-driven desktop publishing software, and one swivel chair! A lot to get used to, but thanks to the computer revolution any number of complicated tasks can be achieved by one person – and quickly.

In the spring of 1983, Microsoft's word processing application, Word, was launched as a supposedly quick and powerful word processor. It was hugely successful and, as it was developed, continued to improve.

It had taken the genius who was at the heart of many of the company's best-selling applications, Charles Simonyi, over a year to finish Word. Like all of Gates's efforts, it was designed to make Microsoft more powerful in the marketplace.

A multi-million-dollar launch

The launch of Microsoft Word cost the company around $3.5 million in free offers, a magazine promotion, and thousands of handouts. This aggressive sales technique fitted Gates's methods well. As part of its expansion, Microsoft had recruited Rowland Hanson onto its management team. Before Microsoft, Hanson had been involved with selling soap products – he knew very little about computers, but he knew how to sell.

Microsoft was making the best products in the computer retail business. Now it had to sell them. Gates needed expert help. Hanson made a simple, but major, decision. He emphasized that it was the name, Microsoft, that people would look for, and trust, if its products were the best, which Gates maintained they were.

Everyone had heard of Microsoft's rival word processing application, WordStar, but hardly anyone knew the company that produced it. Hanson insisted that this would not happen to Microsoft. If a new product was launched with Microsoft's name on it, there would be the expectation of Microsoft excellence. Hanson's thinking was that the brand name gave each product a "halo." So every Microsoft product was marketed with the company name in front of it. Word became Microsoft Word, Excel began life as Microsoft Excel, and so on. It made a real difference and showed just how important it is to have new people in a company to inspire fresh ideas.

Improving

The immediate problem with Microsoft Word in 1983 was that it was not as good as it could be.

It wasn't until the third version, Microsoft Word 3.1, that it began to pay for itself and became a leader in its market. Always anxious to get into the marketplace as soon as possible, Gates had felt that improvements could be made later. He followed the advice of the American General, George S. Patton that "a good plan, violently executed now, is better than a perfect plan next week." If you wait until you have a perfect product, the market may well be gone.

Windows is born

Although Microsoft Word 1.0 was far from perfect, it had one or two new features. The most important was that it had a Graphical User Interface (GUI).

GUI uses words and pictures and icons on the computer screen, instead of the numbers and letters of a text program. It was designed to make computers

"Our success is based on only one thing: good products. It's not very complicated. We're not powerful enough to cause products that are not excellent to sell well."
Bill Gates, 1993.

Bill Gates was determined to make personal computers easily accessible. He realized that in doing so he would create a much bigger market for Microsoft's products. Gates wanted to give all computers a Graphical User Interface (GUI), a simple appearance that would make it obvious how to use the machine. It would be like opening a series of windows to the power of computing, hence its name "WINDOWS."

easier to use. Bill Gates wanted a computer with a GUI. It was one of his visions. He wanted to produce a user-friendly front-end, or appearance to the user, that would make computers accessible to everyone. When a person switches on their computer it is intimidating to be presented with just a flashing marker on a black screen. So Gates insisted that Microsoft begin work on its own GUI operating system to be named Microsoft Windows.

Thirty of its best programmers spent two years developing a product that originally was very poor. In terms of their overall time, they spent something like eighty work-years designing, writing, and testing Windows. But Bill Gates had a vision.

He wanted something that would not only look good and be friendly, but would also enable users to be more efficient. Gates wanted a system that would allow the user to move between different applications easily, and he wanted it to be run with a "mouse." The mouse, again devised to make operating a computer easy, is a small, hand-held unit that, when moved around on a flat pad, moves an arrow to the required position on the screen.

Announcing in advance

Gates made deals, and kept rivals at bay, by announcing Microsoft Windows and other products months in advance of their real launch dates.

One magazine called these incompleted products "vaporware." Announcing in this way meant that if customers were aware that Microsoft was launching a product in the near future, they would wait rather than buy a rival's product. This could be seen by some as unfair trading. But it worked at the time of Windows because many of Microsoft's rivals were producing their own GUI applications – and they were ahead of Microsoft. Gates did not want Microsoft left behind.

However, he now ran into trouble with IBM which wanted to

One of the most difficult things about using a computer is the old-fashioned typewriter keyboard. If the computer has a Graphical User Interface (GUI), then a pointer on the screen can be moved to a picture of what you want, and a button clicked to make the choice. The device to move the pointer and click on the choice is called a mouse – because the 1963 original version appeared to scuttle around and had buttons that looked like ears. In 1983, Microsoft was the first company to bring out the mouse we know today. The plural of the computer mouse is "mouses" rather than "mice."

launch its own GUI application. In a violent reaction, Gates made deals with twenty-four other computer makers stressing that they should support Microsoft Windows rather than the rival IBM application. The relationship with IBM was beginning to unravel. IBM was not as influential in the industry as it had hoped. Microsoft was in charge of everything that happened on the IBM personal computer. IBM was losing even on the computer itself because IBM personal computer clones were making up at least 60% of the computer market.

It was important for IBM to take control once again. It decided that the time was right to produce an updated version of Microsoft's operating system, MS-DOS, and run IBM's own GUI application on it. Microsoft was responsible for updating MS-DOS. Gates said he would – but continued to work on Microsoft Windows as well.

Microsoft pressure

Bill Gates continued to work at a fanatical pace and to expect the same from those around him. He did not want to slow down, or want others to do so either. His average working week was sixty-five hours. When he wasn't working, he might be reading. He loved to read other company success stories – and learn from them – along with biographies of great scientists, politicians and other business executives. In the first five years of the company, Gates took two three-day breaks. In the mid-1980s, he increased that to just one week a year, and, to celebrate Microsoft going public, he even hired a yacht for four days. It just came naturally to him to immerse himself in his work.

Many of those who went to Microsoft got caught up in the ethos, but it didn't always work. The pace at Microsoft had its casualties. One of the senior programmers had been working one-hundred-hour weeks – and was subject to Gates's pressure and short temper as well. After a few months, he had heart failure and had to leave. As a senior executive said later, "You are surrounded with people who are very much the same, and the people who run the

Bill Gates and a former girlfriend. Bill found he had little time for dating when he was so involved with his business. Only later, when Microsoft had fulfilled many of his goals, was he able to turn his attention to personal matters.

Bill Gates was lucky to be able to recruit a friend from his Harvard days, Steve Ballmer, as his closest assistant. Ballmer looked more like a businessman than Gates, but he had the same urge for success and dedication to providing the best products in the shortest possible time. These qualities made him very much a central part of the Microsoft mission.

company are the same, so you just go and go and go. There would be times when people would work more than we wanted them to, and we would try and get them to slow down but sometimes you couldn't get them to stop. When they collapsed you covered them with a blanket and turned off the computer.

"I saw kids, you know, who worked at Microsoft for a few years and truly, I wondered if they would ever be able to work again."

If it wasn't the work schedule that exhausted employees, it might well be Gates's "discussion" technique. It even rebounded on Ballmer – Gates's right-hand man. The delays in getting Windows finished were legendary and significant. Influential magazines were writing that Microsoft had "shot its bolt" and would never be able to deliver its loudly publicized new title. By 1985, Gates was running out of patience and said so – loudly. He warned Ballmer that if there were any more serious delays on Windows then Ballmer would be out of a job. With his company's good name threatened, Gates showed typical ruthlessness.

Microsoft goes public

One of the options available to a successful company is to "go public" and become incorporated, or a public limited company (PLC). This involves asking investors to buy shares in the company so that it is owned, in effect, by a number of different people who expect a return on the money that they have invested in the company. To do this, the company puts its shares on the stock exchange.

In October 1985, Gates, now aged thirty, began to consider this option for Microsoft. The first step in the process is to prepare a prospectus containing a realistic assessment of what the company is worth, what it owns, and a full description of its activities. The prospectus must attract the right investors. If, after being launched on the stock market, the company does not do as well as anticipated, then the people who launched it are liable for anything they failed to show in the prospectus. By January 1986, the Microsoft prospectus was ready.

Bill Gates had many misgivings about going public. One national business law in the States is that when more than five hundred employees have been offered stock as a financial incentive a company must go public. Microsoft would reach the magic five hundred figure sometime in 1986. It had to go public. Gates was concerned that senior programmers who had invested in stock would be watching their stock investment rather than concentrating on their work. He also realized that even more of his precious time would be spent in bookkeeping.

On March 13, 1986, Microsoft was launched on the stock exchange. Because of the value of the shares they held, Gates and Allen were instantly millionaires. By March 1987, the stock had soared in value and Gates was officially a billionaire. His wealth was in the amount of Microsoft that he owned rather than in ready money. His salary in 1990 was just $175,000

The New York stock exchange on Wall Street, Manhattan. Fortunes are made and lost every day as traders buy and sell shares in international companies. On March 13, 1986, the valuable Microsoft shares were launched on the stock exchange – and their worth soared immediately.

Above: Drinks were always free of charge at Microsoft and even the cafeterias had windows looking out onto trees, grassland, fountains, or lakes.

Right: Twenty years after Microsoft was formed in a small office above a bank in Albuquerque, it occupied over two hundred acres in Seattle – and many other sites all over the world.

When the new Microsoft headquarters were built, the first four blocks soon became far too small to cope with the expanding work force. Blocks six and seven were necessary immediately. Why no block five? When it came to be built, Bill Gates saw that it would mean a great many beautiful trees would have to be cut down so it was abandoned. New water features were added to make the surroundings as relaxing as possible.

(£98,000) a year. But the "computer nerd" was now the youngest billionaire in the United States. Yet, Bill Gates continued to live exactly as before.

One thing that Gates and Allen did was to pay tribute to the foresight of their old Lakeside School. They owed everything to the school that had first introduced them to the world of computing. The fact that Lakeside had made such a forward-thinking decision at the precise time that Gates and Allen were there shaped the history of the whole computing industry. Gates and Allen donated $2.2 million (£1.4 million) for a new mathematics and science building for the school. It was named the Allen Gates Hall.

Expanding

Gates had always said that he never wanted Microsoft to be a big company. He wanted to keep personal control over the whole organization and he didn't want it to lose its competitive edge.

But by March 1986, Microsoft had to move again because it now had nearly 1,200 employees. It purchased twenty-nine acres of undeveloped parkland just outside Seattle. Four X-shaped buildings were

quickly constructed – two for the software engineers, two for everyone else. The shape was deliberate because it meant that each office had a window that looked out on the leafy surroundings. Each building had its own fast-food store and, as always at Microsoft, all drinks were free.

In the middle of the four buildings was a small artificial lake, which became known as Lake Bill. Even before the complex was finished, it was too

"Nowhere on earth do more millionaires and billionaires go to work every day than do so here – about 2,200 of the 15,000 employees own at least a million dollars' worth of Microsoft stock . . . ."

John Seabrook, from the New Yorker, Jan. 10, 1994.

small. Within a year, the construction of further buildings began. In 1989, just three years after the move, the company bought the whole of the parkland and had twenty-two buildings on 260 acres; the road leading to the park was renamed "Microsoft Way." The buildings had the feel of a college about them. This was intentional. All of the employees were encouraged to make their rooms their own – just as if they were in a dormitory. It was important that those who are worked so hard in the pursuit of excellence should feel at home and relaxed.

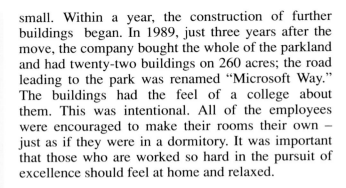

Want to fly, be money-wise, know about dinosaurs or the world of fine art? Microsoft's CD-ROMS make every possible piece of information immediately available. There is no end to the discoveries that information technology allows.

Success breeds enemies

By 1986, Microsoft had started making as many enemies as friends. It had not come up with the updated operating system for IBM. Gates had promised IBM that Microsoft would do it, but he had gone on and produced Windows and allowed the IBM operating system to hang fire – although he had always been careful to back the IBM project in public. IBM was not amused when, in 1990, Windows 3.0 was released and, at last, all that Gates had claimed about his application was true.

This was the next stage of personal computing. Gates was right. IBM was lost. Anyone could buy an IBM personal computer clone and a copy of Windows 3.0. This would give them a better personal computer than buying an IBM even with a different operating system such as Apple's Macintosh.

Gates had made an agreement with Apple some years earlier that Microsoft could use any advances that Apple made in its development of applications. At the time, Apple had no applications of its own, and was dependent on Microsoft's. Gates knew this and when Apple moved into applications, he took on board Apple's advances.

Apple sued Microsoft for copying, claiming that many of the techniques used in Microsoft Windows were a straight copy of the Apple Macintosh design. Gates's determination as he defended his company's reputation is now legendary. Apple got no satisfaction from the lawsuit.

The FTC steps in

However, it came as no surprise that the Federal Trade Commission began an investigation.

The world of computer manufacturing has often been rife with stories of the unethical activities of some of the giants. Microsoft was no exception. Several stories were told to illustrate Gates's technique in trying to steal a march on his rivals. They also showed how close he had come to being unethical – or at least how close others thought he had come.

It was one of these many stories that came to the attention of the FTC. Intuit was a relatively small company based in California whose business was based on a financial applications program. Bill Gates was anxious for Microsoft to produce a similar financial program.

On Microsoft's behalf a visit was made to the chairman of Intuit, Scott Cook. The first proposal was that Microsoft would acquire Intuit and simply take it over. Cook thought it over and said he was interested. However, after preliminary discussions, Gates decided the deal was too costly and withdrew. But after a few months Microsoft went back to Intuit to discuss the possibility of developing an applications program for Microsoft Windows. After the meeting, Microsoft announced that it would not be making a deal after all and would produce its own application without Intuit's help.

A little later, Microsoft launched its application program, Microsoft Money. The story of how Microsoft had led Intuit along the road with promises and had used its ideas, and then produced its own product, was an immediate response. The only weakness in the accusations was that Scott Cook himself said categorically that Microsoft did nothing wrong at all. Cook made it clear that when Microsoft was at Intuit it learned nothing.

"As far as Bill Gates is concerned, business is war," the FTC hearings heard. The FTC sees nothing wrong in this attitude. Many businesses are founded on just such principles. The FTC acknowledged that Microsoft sold over one hundred million copies of MS-DOS. This led to millions of Microsoft packages running on it. Little wonder that its rivals thought MS-DOS really stands for Microsoft Seeks Domination Over Society.

One of the more bizarre attempts to slow Microsoft down was when Apple and IBM joined forces in 1991 – it was seen as an anti-Microsoft deal. The two biggest personal computer hardware companies joined together to resist the rise of a software supplier. Microsoft's dominance was obvious for all to see. Despite the efforts of others, in 1993 Microsoft reported its eighteenth consecutive year of growth.

Being successful

Successful business people often find their private life gets ignored. If entrepreneurs are to be truly fulfilled they dedicate themselves totally to their work. Bill Gates worked long hours – and ignored practically everything else. He had girlfriends and they all testified that his work was of most importance to him. His plans for a home with tunnels connecting a seven-bedroom house, banqueting hall, movie screen, pool, guesthouse and a parking area for twenty-six cars came second to his business success. It was not money, food, possessions, clothes, or pleasure that mattered – but Microsoft and its success.

It was a testament to his achievements that on January 1, 1994, Bill Gates relaxed enough to get married. At thirty-eight, Bill Gates, one of America's wealthiest bachelors, married one of Microsoft's managers, Melinda French.

All right at the top

Bill Gates was not immune to criticism and bad publicity. The sacrifices he made and the dedication he gave made him successful. His vision and his

Opposite: Success can breed jealousy, and Bill Gates found he spent more and more time defending his business policies and attitudes. Complacency had no place at Microsoft – new challenges confronted the organization from top to bottom.
Below: At the age of thirty-eight, one of the world's most eligible bachelors found someone with whom he could share his enthusiams. Microsoft manager, Melinda French, and Bill Gates cheer on the Seattle Supersonics just weeks before getting married in Hawaii.

The most complicated software is at the fingertips of anyone at school or home. The computer revolution has truly changed everyone's lives and prospects – just as Bill Gates predicted it would.

ability kept him in front of the industry. Despite all this he observed, "I've developed a view that being successful is not a fun thing sometimes. There is just a phenomenon where people don't like a company as successful as ours."

Facing the challenge

New challenges constantly face an industry where technology is still advancing, and Bill Gates had the job of ensuring that his company always stayed one step ahead of his rivals. He had to think of the customers and what they needed. In 1994, Microsoft highlighted education as the major growth area for computers and developed software packages that encouraged creativity and actual computer skills, instead of violence and aggression, for the eight-to-fourteen year age range.

"... the computer revolution is still in its infancy – with great possibilities still in front of us."

Bill Gates, 1993.

This was a step that aimed to turn the computer-user on to a new product – and a more socially acceptable one in a world increasingly full of violence – surely another excellent business decision from Bill Gates and Microsoft.

Important Dates

1955   Oct. 28: William H. Gates III is born in Seattle, Washington, in the United States.

1967   Bill Gates goes to Lakeside School.

1968   Lakeside School decides to invest in computer time for its students.

1969   Bill Gates teams up with Paul Allen and two other classmates to form The Lakeside Programmers Group.

1971   The Lakeside Programmers Group writes a payroll program for a local business, Information Sciences, Inc. This is its first real business deal.

1973   Bill Gates goes to Harvard University, in Cambridge, Massachusetts, in the United States.

1974   Dec.: Paul Allen sees an article about a home computer kit, the Altair 8800, in *Popular Electronics*. Allen and Gates contact Ed Roberts of MITS to say they have a form of the computer language, BASIC.

1975   Feb.: The BASIC is finished and later in the year, Gates and Allen sign a deal with MITS.
April: Nineteen year old Gates and Allen set up Microsoft in its own building in Albuquerque, New Mexico, in the United States.

1977   Jan.: At the age of twenty-one, Bill Gates drops out of Harvard University. Microsoft is released from its contract with MITS and owns its BASIC outright. Bill Gates and Microsoft make an agreement with Kuzuhiko Nishi for future developments in Japan.

1979   Jan. 1: Due to the growth of the company, Microsoft moves to new premises in Seattle, in the United States.

1980   Microsoft and the computer manufacturing company IBM make a deal regarding languages and operating systems for IBM's new range of personal computers.

1981   Microsoft signs a deal with Seattle Computer Products to license Q-DOS, later buying the operating system outright.
Microsoft's MS-DOS is introduced onto IBM personal computers.
Bill Gates decides that Microsoft should be in the applications market.

1982   Paul Allen is diagnosed as having Hodgkin's disease.

1983   For health reasons, Paul Allen decides to leave Microsoft.
April: Microsoft introduces a hand-held pointer tool, the mouse, for use in computing.
Sept.: Microsoft's first applications program, WORD 1, is launched.
Nov.: Bill Gates announces that Microsoft will launch a new way to use a computer with a Graphical User Interface (GUI) known as Windows.

1986   March 13: Microsoft is launched on the stock exchange; Gates and Allen become instant millionaires.
Aug.: Bill Gates and Paul Allen donate $2.2 million (£1.4 million) to Lakeside School for a new science and mathematics building, which becomes known as the Allen Gates Hall.
With over 1,200 employees, Microsoft has to move again to bigger premises.

1990	May: Microsoft Windows 3.0 is launched to great acclaim. July: The Microsoft Corporation becomes the first personal computer software company to exceed over $1 billion in sales in a single year.
1992	April: Microsoft is completely successful in its lawsuit with Apple. The final judgment is made, in support of Microsoft, in June 1993. June: Bill Gates accepts the National Medal of Technology from President George Bush.
1993	Jan.: Microsoft becomes the world's largest computer-industry company based on the total value of its stock, a measure known as market value. March: Microsoft moves forward in the educational computer software market by announcing five new multimedia titles; each one is intended to promote the use of multimedia in education.
1994	Jan. 1: Bill Gates, aged thirty-eight, marries one of Microsoft's marketing managers, Melinda French, on Lanai, Hawaii.

Glossary

Applications: *Programs* that are specially written to make computers perform particular tasks. For example, different application packages can turn the computer into a *word processor,* a database, or enable it to lay out spreadsheets for accounting work.

BASIC: **B**eginner's **A**ll-purpose **S**ymbolic **I**nstruction **C**ode is a simple and universal computer programming *language*. It was developed in 1964 and is very popular with amateur programmers because it is fairly easy to learn.

Bug: A bug is a mistake in a computer *program* or system that makes the computer stop working. Some bugs cause the *program* to fail immediately, while others remain dormant until a certain function triggers the bug. Bugs can be introduced into a system on purpose.

Clone: An exact copy of something already in existence. In this case, it

relates to copies of well-known brands of computers and computer *software*. IBM computers have been copied, or cloned, more than any other brand.

COBOL: **CO**mmon **B**usiness-**O**riented **L**anguage is a computer programming language designed for business use.

Commercial: When something is commercial, the intention is to make a profit.

Computer language: Any set of instructions written in a short, simplified group of words or numbers that a computer has been told to recognize through its *operating system*. There are several forms of computer language that different computers are programmed to understand; these include *BASIC, COBOL, FORTRAN,* and Pascal.

Crash: When a computer *program* suddenly fails and stops in the middle of a task or *program*.

Database: An organized store of information used for computer processing.

Disk: A device that stores information for computers on plates that have been coated with a magnetic layer.

Entrepreneur: A person with a sharp *commercial* sense who is prepared to take risks in setting up a new business with a view to making a profit.

Executive: A person in a position of authority within a business or company.

FORTRAN: A simple, universal computer programming *language*. It is very popular with scientists because it can be used to work out complicated formulas. It is short for Formula Translation.

Front-end: The beginning of a *program;* the part of the *program* that appears on the screen as soon as the machine is switched on.

Graphical User Interface (GUI): Where *icons* and menus are shown on a control bar on the screen of a computer. The operator uses a pointer tool, usually a *mouse,* to select the command needed, which appears in rectangular boxes called *windows.* The system was developed to make computing easier by being able to give commands through the control bar as opposed to the complicated way of using codes and numbers.

Hacking: The activities of a computer enthusiast who uses a computer as a hobby. A hacker is, also, someone who tries to gain illegal access to secret information by breaking into company or government computer systems.

Hardware: All the equipment, such as the mechanical and electronic parts of a computer, including the disk drive and the visual display unit of a *personal computer.*

Icon: A small picture on the control bar on the screen of a computer. The user can simply click onto the picture, which represents a function, instead of having to type in a command.

Incorporated (public limited company): Refers to a company formed by several owners. Each owner is responsible, by law, for only a limited amount of the company's debts.

Insomniac: Someone who is unable to sleep.

IQ (Intelligence Quotient): A number that shows a person's mental and academic ability. This is obtained by the person taking an intelligence test. The score of this is then related to the person's age – the ratio of the two numbers, multiplied by one hundred, gives the IQ.

Licensing: The granting of the right to use a product, in this instance, computer *software.*

Market: In terms of a

company's sales plan, it is the number of people who might want to buy a particular item; it also means to sell the item in an organized and preplanned way.

Monopoly: The domination of one company over the selling of a particular product or service, or one particular *market,* to the extent that it is difficult for other companies to compete. This can mean that the dominant company is able to set its own price level and keep the price unreasonably high because it is the only business providing the product or service. There are laws against a company having a monopoly in this way.

Mouse: A small, hand-held device used to select the commands given to the computer. The mouse controls an arrow that appears on the computer screen and is used to point at the *icon* or function of the user's choice. The user clicks onto the *icon* to activate the command.

Operating system: A *program* of instructions stored on the computer's disk drive, or on a *disk,* that tells the computer how to carry out all the basic tasks it has to perform. These include communicating with the user, organizing the filing and running other *programs.*

Personal computer (PC): A small, powerful, desktop computer. The personal computer has become widely accepted in both the home and the workplace. The other types of computer are the mainframe and the mini computers. The mainframe is a bigger computer, with a huge memory capacity, and is generally used by large organizations for many operators to use at once. The mini computer is smaller than a mainframe but bigger than the personal computer.

Profit: The money, in a business deal, that is left over once any costs have been paid.

Program: A list of instructions and codes that control the operation of a computer.

Prospectus: A printed pamphlet detailing the activities and achievements of a business.

Royalty: A fee payable to the owner for the right to use a new invention.

Share: An equal part of a company's capital (overall wealth) that can be bought and owned by a member of the company. If a person buys a share, he or she is then entitled to a percentage of the company's profits.

Software: The computer *programs* and procedures that make the computer perform specific functions and tasks. It is necessary to have *software* to make a computer function at all.

Stock exchange: The place where shares in different companies are bought and sold.

Teletype: A machine that uses electronic signals to send and receive messages. When receiving a message, it converts the signal into print.

Windows: A facility on the later computer *software programs* in which a rectangular area on a computer screen displays a menu of commands or functions. A number of windows can be opened at one time. The purpose of Windows is to make computers more user-friendly.

Word processor: A *software program* designed specifically to work with text – inputting, correcting, and printing words.

Work ethos: A set of ideas or attitudes about how to work and behave that is shared by everyone in a company.

Index